Station 4

150 m diving

150 m diving

800 m. Clambering over boulders and waist-deep water

Entrance

Section where Chris Jewell lost the line

Chamber 3

Diving operations began from here.

Thai Navy SEALs moved the boys between chamber 3 and the entrance.

Names and Locations of Divers:

ENTRANCE OF CAVE TO CHAMBER 3
Unnamed Thai Navy SEALs

STATION 5
Connor Roe (UK)
Ivan Karadzic (DAN)
Josh Bratchley (UK)

STATION 6
Jim Warny (IRL)
Erik Brown (CAN)

STATION 8
Craig Challen (AUS)
Claus Rasmussen (DAN)
Mikko Paasi (FIN)

WITH BOYS
Rick Stanton (UK)
John Volanthen (UK)
Jason Mallinson (UK)
Chris Jewell (UK)
Dr. Richard Harris (AUS)
Four unnamed Thai Navy SEALs

Map Source: Rescue Diver Chris Jewell

TITAN and the WILD BOARS

The True Cave Rescue of the Thai Soccer Team

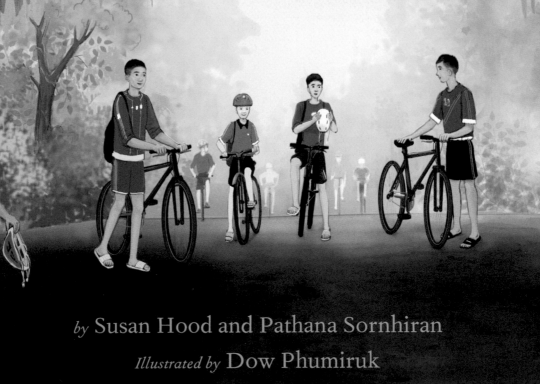

by Susan Hood and Pathana Sornhiran

Illustrated by Dow Phumiruk

HARPER

An Imprint of HarperCollinsPublishers

QUOTE ATTRIBUTIONS

Page 3: The Buddha (Samyutta Nikāya)
Bodhi, Bhikkhu. *The Connected Discourses of the Buddha: A New Translation of the Samyutta Nikāya* (Boston: *Wisdom Publications*, 2000)

Page 5: http://www.dailymail.co.uk/news/article-5940187/Magical-moment-grandmother-aunt-learn-Titan-freed-18-days-underground.html

Page 9: Press conference: https://www.youtube.com/watch?v=62TWYuFn6xM
Video: https://www.wsj.com/articles/thailand-boys-recount-their-ordeal-in-cave-1531922987?ns=prod/accounts-wsj

Page 11: Press conference: https://www.youtube.com/watch?v=62TWYuFn6xM

Page 15: The Buddha (Samyutta Nikāya)
"Sedaka Sutta: At Sedaka" (SN 47.19), translated from the Pali by Thanissaro Bhikkhu. *Access to Insight (BCBS Edition)*, November 30, 2013,
http://www.accesstoinsight.org/tipitaka/sn/sn47/sn47.019.than.html

Page 22: https://www.youtube.com/watch?v=6Rc0ztpAqu0

Page 25: The Buddha (The Dhammapada: The Buddha's Path of Wisdom)
"Kodhavagga: Anger" (Dhp XVII), translated from the Pali by Acharya Buddharakkhita. *Access to Insight (BCBS Edition)*, November 30, 2013,
http://www.accesstoinsight.org/tipitaka/kn/dhp/dhp.17.budd.html

Pages 26-27: Source for all letters (Translated by Pathana Sornhiran): https://www.bbc.com/news/world-asia-44748927

Page 41: https://www.washingtonpost.com/world/thai-authorities-prepare-to-rescue-remaining-four-boys-and-their-coach-from-a-flooded-cave-as-the-eight-freed-boys-start-laughing-joking-with-doctors/2018/07/10/1af52f52-83b5-11e8-9e06-4db52ac42e05_story.html?utm_termh

Page 42: The Buddha (the Mettā Sutta)
"Karanīya Mettā Sutta: The Discourse on Loving-kindness" (Sn 1.8), translated from the Pali by Piyadassi Thera. *Access to Insight (BCBS Edition)*,
August 29, 2012, http://www.accesstoinsight.org/tipitaka/kn/snp/snp.1.08.piya.html

Page 44: Press conference: https://www.youtube.com/watch?v=62TWYuFn6xM (Translated by Pathana Sornhiran)
Interview: https://www.npr.org/2018/07/11/627978899/after-achieving-mission-possible-thai-boys-seen-recovering-happily-in-new-video

Page 46: https://www.nytimes.com/2018/07/10/world/asia/thailand-cave-rescue-how.html

Page 48: https://www.cnn.com/2018/07/11/asia/thai-cave-rescue-father-interview/index.html

Titan and the Wild Boars: The True Cave Rescue of the Thai Soccer Team
Text copyright © 2019 by Susan Hood and Pathana Sornhiran
Illustrations copyright © 2019 by Dow Phumiruk
All rights reserved. Printed in the United States of America.
No part of this book may be used or reproduced in any manner whatsoever without written permission except in the case of
brief quotations embodied in critical articles and reviews. For information address HarperCollins Children's Books,
a division of HarperCollins Publishers, 195 Broadway, New York, NY 10007.
www.harpercollinschildrens.com

Library of Congress Control Number: 2018964879
ISBN 978-0-06-290772-1

The artist used pencil, charcoal, and ink sketches and Photoshop to create the digital illustrations for this book.
Typography by Dana Fritts
19 20 21 22 23 PC 10 9 8 7 6 5 4 3 2 1

❖

First Edition

For Saman Kunan,
who gave his life to rescue the boys

*"We will develop and cultivate the liberation of mind
by loving-kindness, make it our vehicle, make it our basis,
stabilize it, exercise ourselves in it, and fully perfect it."*
—The Buddha (Samyutta Nikāya)

Like his friends in Mae Sai and many kids in Thailand, eleven-year-old Chanin grew up obsessed with soccer. He started playing at age six and joined the Wild Boars team a couple of years later.

Chanin's family nicknamed him Titan after the powerful giants of Greek mythology. Little Titan may not have measured up in height, but like these gods, he was known for his strength. "He is small but very tough," said his aunt. "His coach said he plays like a boy aged fourteen. Whenever he gets knocked down, he just jumps up straightaway."

At first, Titan didn't even own soccer shoes. He played in a friend's hand-me-downs, wrapped together in duct tape. He saved 300 baht from his pocket money to buy his own.

As one of the youngest members of the Wild Boars, Titan trained hard to play striker. Riding his bike for miles on rugged mountain roads in Thailand's steamy heat was just part of the drill.

DAY 1

One Saturday after soccer practice, Titan, his friends, and Coach Ek rode their bikes to explore a favorite cave six miles away. They dropped their bikes, ignoring the sign outside the cave that warned visitors not to enter during the monsoon season starting in July. It was still June, after all, and a few of them had been there before. The storied "hidden city" within the cave excited the boys eager for adventure, and the cool, dark secret passages beckoned.

Titan and his friends ventured deep into the cave, sloshing through muddy water, rounding dripping stalactites and jagged stalagmites, squeezing through tight passages. Little did they know that outside it had begun to rain. Hard.

When the boys turned to go home, water was streaming down the porous limestone walls of the cave and bubbling up from the ground, flooding the tunnel back to the entrance.

The boys asked their coach, "How are we going to get out of here?"

"Don't be scared," said Coach Ek. "Someone will come and find us." He led the boys deeper into the cave to a ledge where they could rest until morning. Surely the water level would drop by then.

That night, worried parents reported their sons missing.

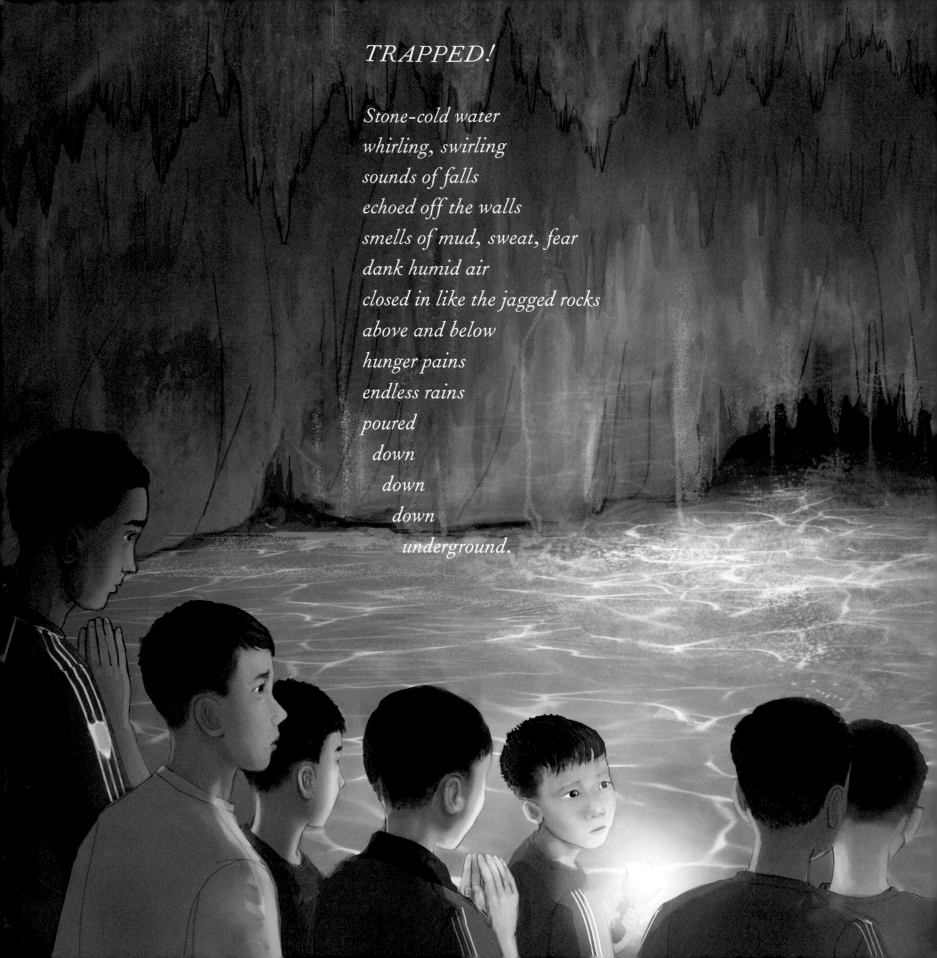

TRAPPED!

Stone-cold water
whirling, swirling
sounds of falls
echoed off the walls
smells of mud, sweat, fear
dank humid air
closed in like the jagged rocks
above and below
hunger pains
endless rains
poured
  down
    down
      down
        underground.

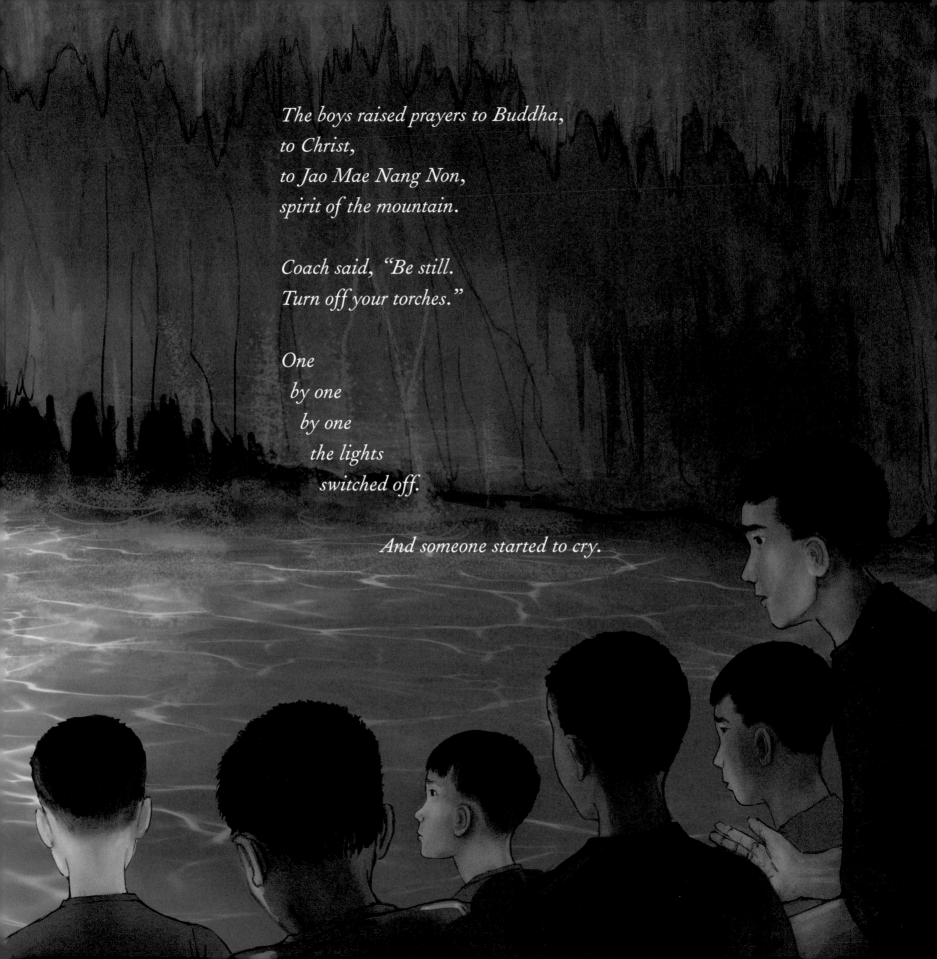

The boys raised prayers to Buddha,
to Christ,
to Jao Mae Nang Non,
spirit of the mountain.

Coach said, "Be still.
Turn off your torches."

One
　by one
　　by one
　　　the lights
　　　switched off.

　　　　　And someone started to cry.

DAYS 2–5

News of Titan and the trapped boys traveled far and fast. Over the next few days, thousands of soldiers, park rangers, engineers, geologists, doctors, divers, officials, and other volunteers poured in to help, including the Royal Thai Navy SEALs and expert cave divers from around the world.

Pattaya Beach, a higher open cavern where rescuers suspected the boys might be

British spelunker Vernon Unsworth, who lived nearby and had spent more than six years exploring the cave, mapped it for the rescue crew. In total it was 10 km, or 6.2 miles long.

Inside the cave, time inched along . . . day . . . after day . . . after day. Morning was as black as night. It was difficult to sleep perched on the rocky ledge. Titan tried not to think about food, knowing it would only make him hungrier, but one of the boys cried out for congee (rice porridge) in his sleep.

Coach Ek urged Titan and his friends to drink the clean water dripping down the stalactites and taught them to meditate to conserve energy. When they were not resting, the teammates took turns digging to try to find a way out.

As the days passed, Titan grew dizzy, his strength sapping away. He had watched the World Cup with his dad on their last night together. Now he knew his parents and five-year-old brother Toto would be worrying about him. Would anyone ever find them? Coach Ek glanced at him and gave him a hug.

"When watching after others, you watch after yourself."
—The Buddha

DAYS 5—9

Outside, the experts had never faced such a complex and dangerous rescue operation. As the monsoon rains drummed down, the divers crouched, crawled, and swam, fighting mudslides and whirlpools, feeling their way along the flooded pitch-black tunnels. The cold made their teeth chatter when they were able to surface in an air pocket.

Divers scaled boulders the size of a house and slid down
rock cliffs. The current was so strong it could knock divers'
masks from their faces. Silt stirred up in the water made
flashlights nearly useless.

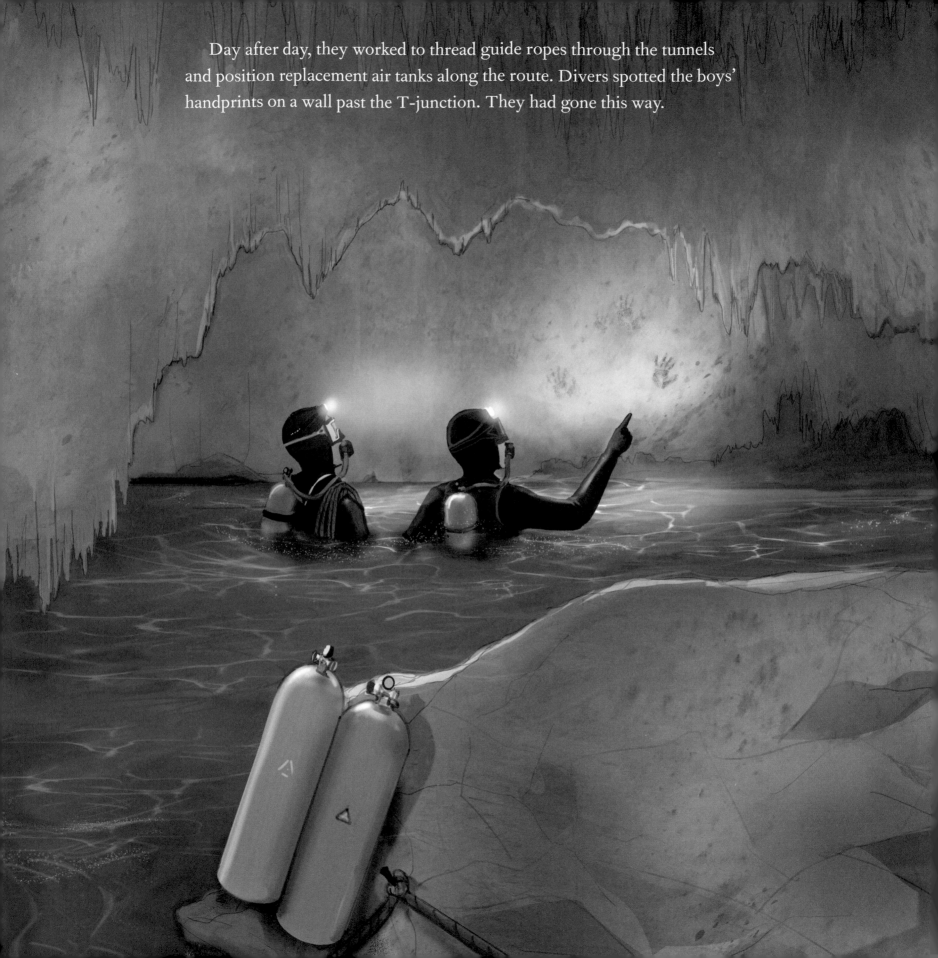

Day after day, they worked to thread guide ropes through the tunnels
and position replacement air tanks along the route. Divers spotted the boys'
handprints on a wall past the T-junction. They had gone this way.

Narrow passages in the rocks (one only fifteen inches high) obstructed progress; the divers could not fit through with their air tanks. Hours went by, and each time the tanks ran low, the divers couldn't just surface to breathe. They were forced to turn back.

Where could the boys be? the divers wondered. How would they find them? And after so many days without food, could they still be alive?

TEDIUM

For the boys, time u . . . n . . . w . . . o . . . u . . . n . . . d
underground
in the dark.
Hours and days replayed
in endless
digging,
meditating,
praying,
digging,
meditating,
praying . . .

Then, wait! What was that? Listen! Strange voices in the dark.
What were they saying? Were the boys hallucinating?
Titan's friend Adul shone a light down the ledge and was stunned
by what he saw.

Two divers!

"How many of you?" asked one, his headlamp illuminating their astonished faces. Adul could barely speak. The diver was not Thai and he was speaking English. As one of the few boys who understood him, Adul answered: "Thirteen."

"Brilliant," said the diver. "Many people are coming. We are the first. You have been here ten days. You are very strong."

Titan and his friends looked from one to another, frustrated that they couldn't understand what was being said. Would they go home now? Did the divers have food?

"Eat, eat, eat!" cried one of the boys.

But food would have to wait until the divers could make the long,

exhausting trip out of the cave and back to them again the following day.

Titan watched the divers slip under the water and disappear into the dark.

"Breaking News!" "Thai Lucky 13 Found!" blared the headlines about the lost-and-now-found boys. Everyone hailed the rescuers as heroes and thanked all the gods in heaven for the boys' safety.

But a bigger problem loomed. None of the boys knew how to scuba dive and they were terribly weak after ten days in the cave without food. How would they get out?

DIVERS FIND BOYS IN CAVE

Thai Boys FOUND

ปลอดภัย
นักดำน้ำเจอทีมหมูป่า

What Next for the Soccer Team Found in Cave?
rescue underway

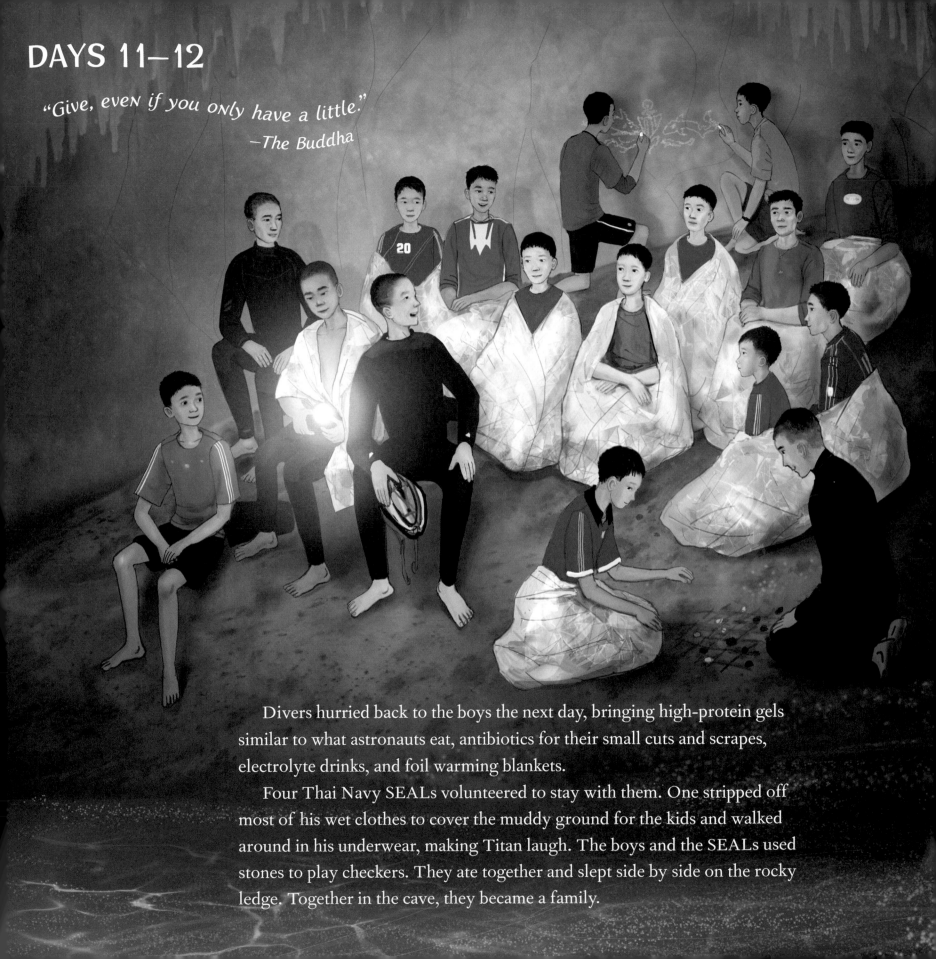

DAYS 11—12

"Give, even if you only have a little."
—The Buddha

Divers hurried back to the boys the next day, bringing high-protein gels similar to what astronauts eat, antibiotics for their small cuts and scrapes, electrolyte drinks, and foil warming blankets.

Four Thai Navy SEALs volunteered to stay with them. One stripped off most of his wet clothes to cover the muddy ground for the kids and walked around in his underwear, making Titan laugh. The boys and the SEALs used stones to play checkers. They ate together and slept side by side on the rocky ledge. Together in the cave, they became a family.

One diver offered the boys waterproof paper to send notes to their parents waiting outside the cave.

Titan wrote,

Dad and Mum, don't worry about me. I'm fine. Tell Yod to get ready to take me to eat fried chicken. Love you.

Coach Ek wrote to his relatives and apologized to the boys' parents.

Dear Aunty and Granny,

I'm doing well. Don't worry about me too much. Please take care of yourselves. Aunty, can you please tell Granny to prepare vegetable juice and pork crackers? I'll eat them when I get out. Love you all.

To all parents, now the kids are fine . . . And I promise I will take care of the kids as best as I can. Thank you for all your support. Please accept my apology.

And the parents wrote back. None of them blamed the boys or the coach, but they urged them to stay strong.

My dear Titan,

Mummy is waiting for you outside the cave. Mummy loves you and misses you so much. You have to be patient and fight. You have to be strong. I'm waiting for you just outside. You have to make it. I believe you can do it. You'll always have Mummy's support. I love you so much.

Daddy also misses you dearly and loves you with all his heart. Love.

Dear Coach Ek,

We parents would like to ask you to look after our children. Don't blame yourself. We want you to rest assured none of us feels angry with you. We all understand and support you. Thank you for looking after our children. Coach, you've gone in there with them. Come out with them too and do it safely.

ลูกอยู่หน้า ถ้าน
กอดทนและสู้น
า ลูกต้อง ทำให้
ใจให้ลูกอยู่เส
รักลูกสุด

ก็บย่า
ผมมา
เอย่า
ก็ไปแ

ถึง โค้ทเอก
พ่อแม่ทุก คนฝากโค้ท เอกดูแล น้อง
โค้ทเอกไม่ต้องโทษตัวเอง
สบายใจพ่อแ

Meanwhile, machines were working overtime in the cave to pump the water out. Hundreds of rescuers were threading more guide ropes into the tunnels, along with three-mile cables to set up video communications between the boys and their parents. Expert divers delivered extra air tanks to have ready along the route.

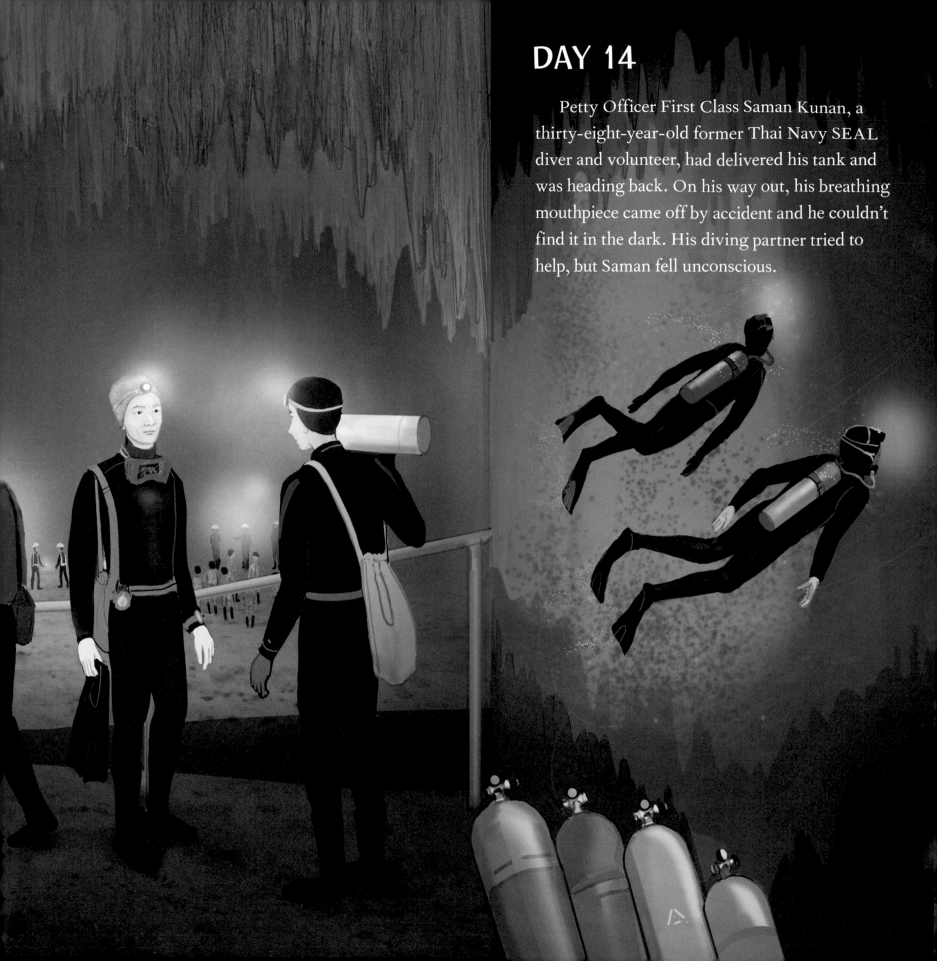

DAY 14

Petty Officer First Class Saman Kunan, a thirty-eight-year-old former Thai Navy SEAL diver and volunteer, had delivered his tank and was heading back. On his way out, his breathing mouthpiece came off by accident and he couldn't find it in the dark. His diving partner tried to help, but Saman fell unconscious.

Saman died.

The tragic news slammed the waiting world, sinking morale to alarming depths. If a triathlete and highly trained diver could die in the cave, what chance would the young coach and twelve half-starved boys have to escape?

DAY 15

New weather forecasts were foreboding; even more rain was expected. If the water levels rose, filling the cave, the boys could drown. Even now, the oxygen level inside the cave had dropped from the usual 21 percent to 15 percent. The rescue commander announced that Sunday, July 8, was D-Day.

They had no choice. Titan and the boys had to get out. NOW!

The world held its breath. Schoolmates sang and prayed for their friends; some folded origami cranes, symbols of luck and long life. Hopes and prayers from around the globe winged their way to the cave.

DAY 16: D-DAY

It was time. Australian doctor Richard Harris dove into the cave to prep the boys for their escape. Given their lack of scuba experience, he explained, a team of thirteen international divers would guide them out.

Who would go first? The strongest? The weakest? The boys decided as a team. Coach Ek had a suggestion: the boys who lived farthest from the caves should go first, because they would have the longest bike ride back home. Little did they know that thousands were waiting outside to welcome and assist them.

Four boys volunteered. Titan waited and watched as they were given sedatives to keep them calm and fitted with full-face masks. One by one, they were whisked off into the water, into the dark.

Would he ever see them again? Titan wondered.

News of success reached Titan and the other boys when the divers returned on Monday, the following day. Four boys were OUT! The divers prepped four more volunteers to leave.

DAY 18

Tuesday dawned with news of a second success. Eight boys were safe! Now it was Titan's turn. Like his friends, Titan was dressed in a wet suit and life jacket with an air cylinder and harness. The doctor gave him a sedative and he fell asleep with a full-face mask providing oxygen.

Following a guide rope bolted into the rocks, one of the best divers in the world shepherded Titan through the black tunnels, dark as deep space. He swam with Titan's head close to his own so he could feel the boy's air bubbles and know he was still breathing.

Up, down, under, and through they went. The diver navigated steep hills and tight passages, feeling his way along. He occasionally smacked his head on the rocks in the pitch black. When the two emerged from the underwater tunnels, additional rescuers strapped Titan in a flexible plastic stretcher called a Sked. They carried him over rocky ground and even used a rope and pulley system to zip the Sked across steep valleys.

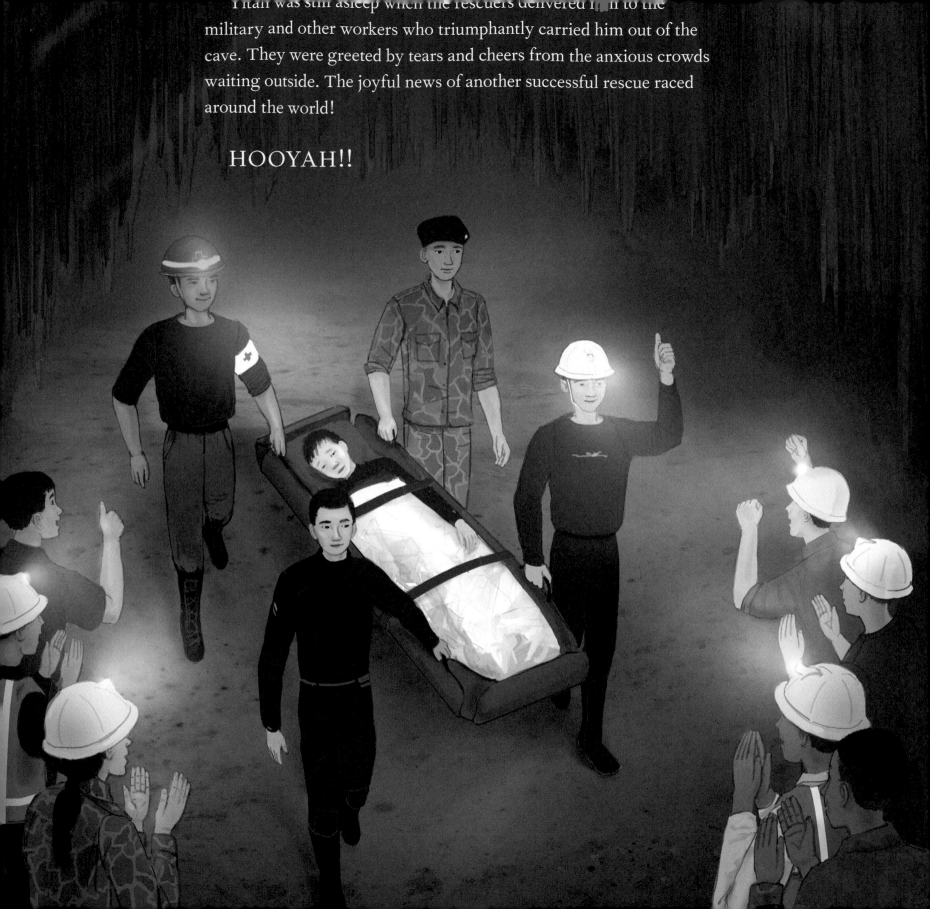

Titan was still asleep when the rescuers delivered him to the military and other workers who triumphantly carried him out of the cave. They were greeted by tears and cheers from the anxious crowds waiting outside. The joyful news of another successful rescue raced around the world!

HOOYAH!!

In the hospital, Titan was reunited with his friends. All twelve boys and their coach were safe! He burst into tears when he saw his parents through the glass partition. Happy tears.

What many had called "Mission Impossible" was now "Mission Accomplished." The Thai SEALs said, "We are not sure if this is a miracle, a science, or what. . . ."

Miracle. Science. Patience. Expertise. Luck. Sacrifice. Most of all . . .

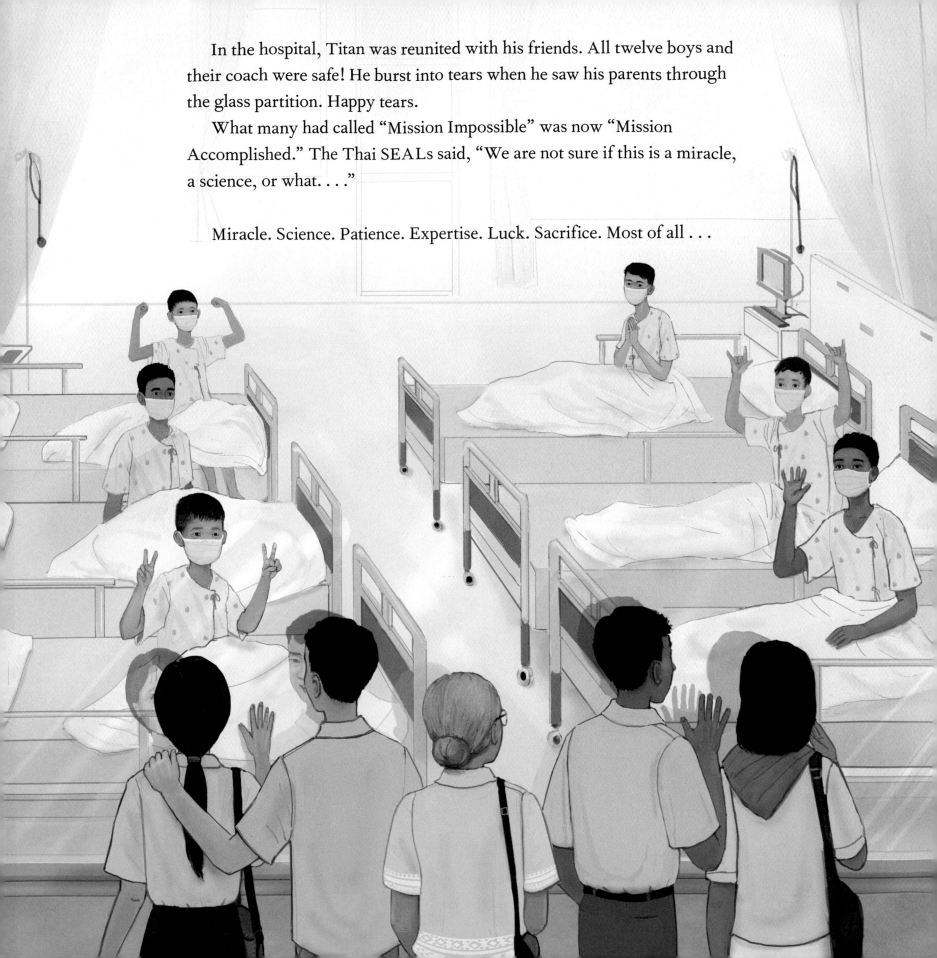

"... radiate boundless love towards the entire world ..."

—The Buddha

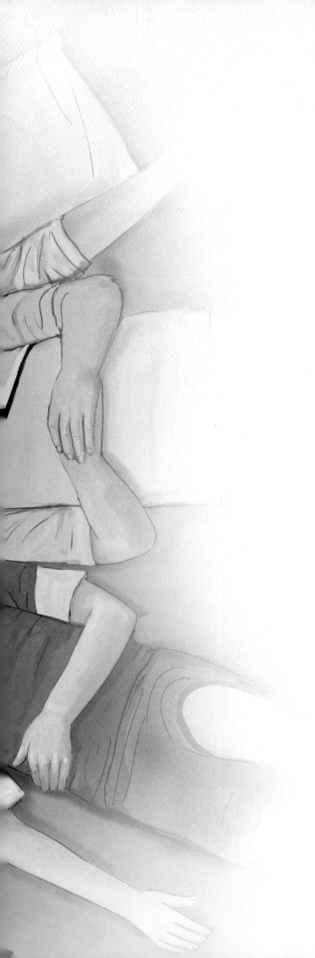

TEAMWORK

Titan and the Wild Boars
played together
strayed together
braved together
caved together
humbled together
crumbled together
stayed together
prayed together
dug together
hugged together
kneeled together
healed together.

Titan and the Wild Boars
brought the world together
as one team,
with loving-kindness
sparking a light in the dark
     for us all.

More About the Cave Rescue

It was Saturday, June 23, 2018, when eleven-year-old Chanin Vibulrungruang, eleven teammates (ages twelve to seventeen), and their twenty-five-year-old coach entered the Tham Luang Nang Non Caves in the northern province of Chiang Rai, Thailand. Most of the boys had told their parents they were going to play soccer (known as "football" in Thailand) but not about the cave they planned to visit afterward. They intended to explore for only an hour or so. By nightfall, they had not come home. Songpul Kanthawong (age thirteen), a teammate who hadn't had his bike and so was unable to join the trip, told the frantic parents about the caves.

When Coach Ek realized his team was trapped, he advised the boys to save the batteries in their flashlights ("torches") and led them in prayer and meditation he had learned apprenticing as a Buddhist monk. They spent the next ten days perched on a high ledge deep inside the cave.

On July 2, British cave divers John Volanthen and Rick Stanton, considered among the best in the world, found the boys alive. They were laying guidelines when they came to an air pocket. They surfaced and Stanton smelled the boys before he saw them. There they were, crawling down the sloping ledge toward them.

Now how to get them out? Drilling down into the mountain would take too long; teaching the weakened boys to scuba dive through the treacherous passageways seemed impossible. Some suggested waiting until the rainy season was over in November. That would leave the boys in the caves for four months! In the end, the decreasing level of oxygen in the cave triggered a decision. If it went down to 12 percent, the boys could experience vomiting, loss of consciousness, convulsions, and cardiac arrest.

Sunday, July 8, was declared D-Day. At ten a.m. local time, a team of international divers entered the cave to rescue four boys. The first boy emerged at 5:40 p.m., the second at 5:50 p.m., the third at 7:40 p.m., and the fourth at 7:50 p.m. Ambulances rushed them to helicopters, where they were airlifted to the Chiang Rai Prachanukroh Hospital, thirty-seven miles away. Authorities did not release the names of the four boys, and parents were not yet allowed to visit them. Doctors kept them in quarantine until they made sure the boys had not contracted any infectious diseases from contaminated water or bat droppings inside the cave.

The rescue of the second group of boys would have to wait until morning. The divers were too exhausted to conduct more than one rescue each day.

On Monday, July 9, four more boys were successfully evacuated in nine hours. Once again, their names were not released.

Titan was evacuated on Tuesday, July 10, with his coach and three remaining teammates. The final boy was evacuated with four SEALs, including an army doctor. In the end, forty Thai and fifty international divers had been deployed.

As rescue operations wound down, there was one last moment of peril. The main pump in the cave malfunctioned and the water level surged, forcing final personnel in the cave to scramble for their lives. All survived.

In the hospital, the boys recovered for about a week, waving to their parents behind glass windows. A few had suffered minor lung and ear infections, but all emerged healthy for their eagerly awaited news conference on July 18.

After a short time at home, eleven of the boys entered the Buddhist monkhood, living in a temple for nine days to train as novices to honor the memory of Saman Kunan, the diver who died to save them. (Adul did not participate because he is Christian.) Their coach, who had already served as a novice for ten years, was ordained as a monk.

Today, the boys are back home, going to school and playing soccer. "This experience has made me more patient, stronger, and less easily discouraged," said Titan. Like many of his teammates, Titan now hopes to grow up to be a professional soccer player.

"I want to say thanks to those who rescued my boy," said Titan's father. "And helped him to have a new life—it's like a rebirth."

AP Photo/Vincent Thian

Boys—upper row from left to right: Nickname/Full name: Night/Peerapat Sompiangjai; Nick/Pipat Bodhi; Note/Prajak Sutham; Mick/Panumas Sangdee; Tie/Nattavut Takhamsong; Pong/Somphong Jaiwong. *Boys—front row from left to right:* Coach Ek/Ekapol Chanthawong (standing); Tee/Pornchai Kamluang; Adul/Adul Sam-on; Titan/Chanin Vibulrungruang; Mark/Monkol Boonpeam; Biw/Ekarat Wongsookchan; Dom/Duangpech Promthep. *Note: Thai names can be spelled in different ways when translated into English.*

Fascinating Facts

• Four boys missed their birthdays while in the cave: Nick and Night (June 23), Note (July 1), and Dom (July 3).

• Many of the boys, including Titan, had cell phones with them, but there was no reception in the cave.

• Coach Ek was orphaned at an early age, losing both his parents and brother to disease. He trained as a monk but left the monastery to care for his ill grandmother.

• The Wild Boars owe their lives in part to two "Wet Mules"—that's the name of rescuers Dr. Richard Harris and Craig Challen's expert dive group in Australia.

• Divers tested masks and wet suits on local schoolchildren in a pool.

• Contrary to many news reports, diver Chris Jewell said that the plastic stretchers called Skeds were not used in the underwater sections of the cave rescue. And in the end, one diver (not two as originally planned) accompanied each boy out of the cave to avoid bottlenecks.

• Rescue assistance came from countries around the world, including Australia, Belgium, Canada, China, the Czech Republic, Denmark, Finland, Germany, India, Ireland, Israel, Japan, Laos, Myanmar, the Netherlands, the Philippines, Russia, Singapore, Spain, Sweden, Ukraine, the United Kingdom, and the United States.

The Wild Boars

The Wild Boars (*Moo Pa* in Thai) got their name in honor of founder Kamol Chanthapoon's family's pig and cattle ranch in 2016. The players (ages eleven to seventeen) go to different schools; no one is turned away from the team, including several boys who are known as "stateless" (not recognized as citizens of any country). Those boys come from neighboring countries near the infamous "Golden Triangle"—a region known for drug smuggling bordering Myanmar, Laos, and Thailand. The boys devote themselves to soccer, and their hard work has paid off. They won a regional tournament in May 2018. Head coach Nopparat Kanthawong hopes to train the boys to play for professional teams.

Stateless No More

Three of the boys (Pornchai Kamluang, Adul Sam-on, and Monkol Boonpeam) and their coach, Ekapol Chanthawong, were among the estimated 480,000 people regarded as "stateless" ethnic minorities who live around the borders of Thailand, Myanmar, Laos, and China. As such, the boys and their coach had few rights in Thailand. They could go to school but could not open bank accounts, get a job, obtain a passport, buy land, marry, or vote legally. On August 8, 2018, the three Wild Boars and their coach were granted Thai citizenship. Now they are free to pursue their dreams and try to be all they want to be.

Legend of the Tham Luang Nang Non Caves

Many believe that spirits inhabit the caves of Thailand. According to Thai folklore, the spirit of Jao Mae Nang Non (a princess who fell in love with a stableboy) lingers in the cave; she died there mourning her true love after her father killed him. Legend says that water flowing in the cave is her blood and the surrounding mountain is her sleeping body. A shrine to the princess appears near the mouth of the cave. Some suggest it was Coach (and former monk) Ek's prayers to Buddha that stilled the restless spirit and led to the boys' successful escape.

Timeline: June to July 2018

SATURDAY, JUNE 23: Boys enter the cave and become trapped by monsoon rains flooding the tunnels. Parents report them missing. The boys' bicycles, backpacks, and shoes are found.

SUNDAY, JUNE 24: Frantic relatives and local officials gather outside the cave.

MONDAY, JUNE 25: Thai Navy SEALs begin searching the tunnels.

TUESDAY, JUNE 26: Divers reach the T-junction, but rising waters force them to turn back.

WEDNESDAY, JUNE 27: International cave-diving experts join the rescue operation.

THURSDAY, JUNE 28: Operations are suspended because of floods filling the cave. Drilling begins to try to drain water. Drones look for vents in the mountaintop.

FRIDAY, JUNE 29: Thailand prime minister Prayut Chan-ocha visits the cave to boost morale and pledge the country's support.

SATURDAY, JUNE 30: Rains stop and divers swim deeper into the tunnels.

SUNDAY, JULY 1: Rescuers set up a relatively dry staging area called Chamber 3. Hundreds of air tanks and other supplies are delivered there.

MONDAY, JULY 2: A miracle! Two British cave divers discover the boys alive late Monday evening.

TUESDAY, JULY 3: Divers deliver food, water, blankets, and medicine to the boys as rescuers weigh different plans to get the boys out.

WEDNESDAY, JULY 4: Divers deliver additional food supplies.

THURSDAY, JULY 5: Divers continue to thread guide ropes through the cave and station replacement air tanks along the route. Pumps continue to drain water from the caves.

FRIDAY, JULY 6: Tragedy strikes. Former elite Navy SEAL diver Saman Kunan dies. Decreasing oxygen levels in the cave and worsening forecasts trigger the decision to get the boys out.

SATURDAY, JULY 7: Discussions continue about best possible evacuation strategies. Divers practice rescue techniques in a swimming pool.

SUNDAY, JULY 8: D-Day! Expert divers spend eleven hours rescuing the first four boys.

MONDAY, JULY 9: Four more boys are rescued.

TUESDAY, JULY 10: The last four boys, including Titan, and their coach are saved!

"It was eighteen days, but it felt like years."
—Prayuth Jetiyanukarn, abbot at temple where Coach Ek works

Interview with British Divers Chris Jewell and Jason Mallinson

Chris Jewell and Jason Mallinson are part of the "awesome foursome" of divers from the British Cave Rescue Council charged with guiding the sedated boys through the underwater tunnels in the caves. Chris and Jason each conveyed one boy out of the cave each day, as did their fellow divers John Volanthen and Rick Stanton. (Jason also helped evacuate the coach on the final day.) A team of divers from Australia, Canada, Ireland, Denmark, Finland, and Thailand provided additional support. I talked with Chris and Jason to understand the special dangers of their mission.

Susan Hood: Had you ever experienced a rescue situation like this before?

Chris Jewell: The situation in the Thai caves was unprecedented. Nothing like this has ever happened before in terms of the distance we had to travel with each of the boys and difficult cave conditions—constricted passages with almost zero visibility in the water. While we are used to getting ourselves through caves like this, bringing another person through this cave was difficult and extremely risky. We never thought we'd have a one hundred percent success rate.

SH: When you first met the boys, did any of them seem worried about making the trip out of the cave?

CJ: No. None of them showed any signs of stress or anxiety. They did everything correctly to help us. They were incredibly brave.

SH: Both you and Jason faced terrifying situations shepherding the last boys out.

CJ: Yes. I was guiding the second-to-last boy out when I lost my grip on the guideline and couldn't find it again. I spent about four minutes in the pitch black searching for it. Finally, I found an electrical cable, but it led me the wrong way, back into the cave. I waited there with the boy until Jason came along and helped me find the guide rope again.

Jason Mallinson: The final boy to leave was much smaller than we had expected, and consequently the full-face mask that we had brought for him did not fit his face. It was too big. We spent quite a while trying this mask and a smaller one, which was not as robust. Nevertheless, time was pressing, the rains were getting stronger, and we had to make the critical decision to get him out at that moment, rather than wait another day (or in fact never be able to get back to him). We decided on the smaller mask and took each dive section at a much slower pace. There was little, if any, visibility due to the muddy water. It was a nervous time. I kept his face very close and just below mine, and so if we hit the walls or roof, which was inevitable (due to the poor visibility), my head always hit first, thus protecting his. Despite this, the recovery dive went well. I was relieved to deliver the healthy boy to the medical team about three hours later.

SH: How did you feel when the last boy made it out alive?

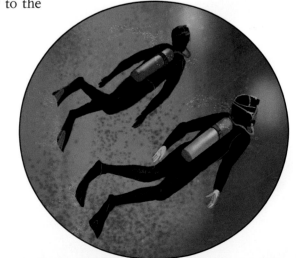

CJ: When the last of the boys came out of the water it was a great relief. However, we didn't celebrate until the last of the rescue workers had exited the cave. The rescue was a tremendous international effort where the whole world came together to make this possible. We feel proud to have played our part in this team.

Authors' note: For weeks, the Thai government did not release information about the order in which the boys were rescued. Later reports say it was the team's decision to save members of this last group in this order: Coach Ek, Tee, Titan, Pong, and finally Mark.

AP Photo/Vincent Thian

Saman Kunan—A Real-Life Superhero

While in the hospital, the boys wept to learn of thirty-eight-year-old Saman Kunan, a former elite Thai Navy SEAL who died around one a.m. on Friday, July 6, 2018, in his effort to rescue them. One of Titan's relatives drew this portrait of him; the boys and their families wrote messages of condolence around it. Titan's family wrote, "Sam is our hero for our family forever. We will not forget." The king of Thailand ordered full honors for Saman's funeral and bestowed upon him the title of lieutenant commander.

Sources and Interesting Websites
For additional sources, visit: hc.com/wildboars

Meet the boys and their rescuers: https://infographics.channelnewsasia.com/interactive/thaicaverescueheroes/index.html

Relive the amazing rescue operation: https://www.channelnewsasia.com/news/topic/Thailand-cave-rescue
https://www.abc.net.au/news/2018-07-13/thai-cave-rescue-tham-luang-extreme-challenges/9985286

Out of the Dark – Behind the Scenes Australian documentary: https://boingboing.net/2018/07/23/an-hour-long-documentary-on-th.html

Cave rescue: Key questions answered: https://www.bbc.com/news/world-asia-44799779

ABC news interview with Titan: https://abcnews.go.com/international/boy-rescued-thai-soccer-team-happy-home/story?id=56682013

Watch the moment the boys are discovered alive: https://www.youtube.com/watch?v=6Rc0ztpAqu0

Thai boys' press conference: https://www.youtube.com/watch?v=62TWYuFn6xM

The boys' Buddhist ceremonies: https://www.youtube.com/watch?v=m2EjupeY8-Y

Interview with the boys weeks after the rescue: https://www.youtube.com/watch?v=Jw0_5UlFwHA

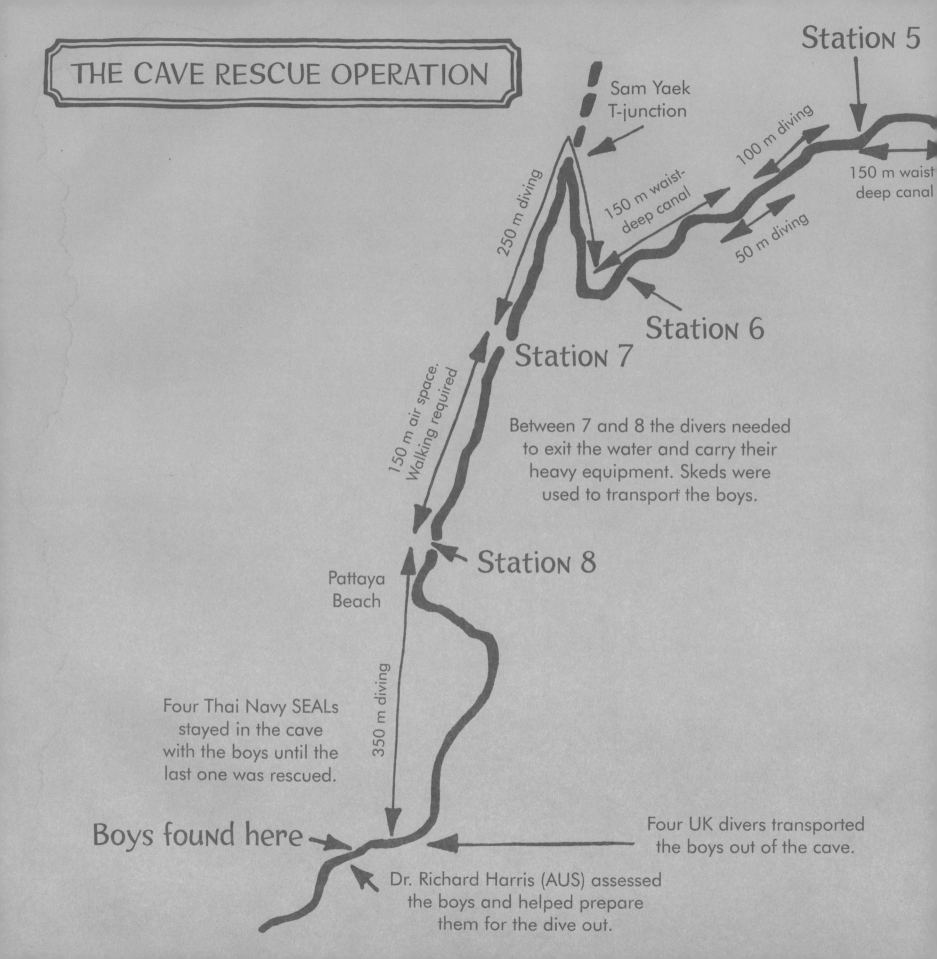

THE CAVE RESCUE OPERATION

Station 5

Sam Yaek
T-junction

100 m diving

150 m waist
deep canal

250 m diving

150 m waist-
deep canal

50 m diving

Station 6

Station 7

150 m air space.
Walking required

Between 7 and 8 the divers needed
to exit the water and carry their
heavy equipment. Skeds were
used to transport the boys.

Station 8

Pattaya
Beach

350 m diving

Four Thai Navy SEALs
stayed in the cave
with the boys until the
last one was rescued.

Boys found here →

Four UK divers transported
the boys out of the cave.

Dr. Richard Harris (AUS) assessed
the boys and helped prepare
them for the dive out.